Deadly NATURE

Camilla de la Bedoyere
Consultant: Steve Parker

Miles Kelly

Please return / renew by date shown.
You can renew it at:
norlink.norfolk.gov.uk
or by telephone: 0344 800 8006
Please have your library card & PIN ready

NORFOLK LIBRARY
AND INFORMATION SERVICE

First published in 2014 by
Miles Kelly Publishing Ltd
Harding's Barn, Bardfield End Green,
Thaxted, Essex, CM6 3PX, UK

Copyright © Miles Kelly Publishing Ltd 2013

© 2014 Discovery Communications, LLC.
Discovery Explore Your World™ and the
Discovery Explore Your World™ logo are
trademarks of Discovery Communications, LLC,
used under license. All rights reserved.
discoveryuk.com

10 9 8 7 6 5 4 3 2 1

Publishing Director Belinda Gallagher
Creative Director Jo Cowan
Managing Editor Amanda Askew
Managing Designer Simon Lee
Senior Editors Carly Blake, Rosie Neave
Proofreader Fran Bromage
Production Manager Elizabeth Collins
Image Manager Liberty Newton
Reprographics Stephan Davis, Thom Allaway

ISBN 978-1-78209-528-6

Printed in China

British Library Cataloguing-in-Publication Data
A catalogue record for this book is available
from the British Library

Made with paper from a sustainable forest

www.mileskelly.net
info@mileskelly.net

ACKNOWLEDGMENTS

The publishers would like to thank the following sources for the use
of their photographs:

KEY A=Alamy B=Bridgeman CO=Corbis D=Dreamstime F=Fotolia FLPA=Frank Lane
Picture Agency GI=Getty Images IS=istockphoto.com N=Newscom NG=National
Geographic NPL=Nature Picture Library P=Photoshot R=Reuters RF=Rex Features
SPL=Science Photo Library S=Shutterstock SS=Superstock TF=Topfoto
t=top, a=above, b=bottom/below, c=center, l=left, r=right, f=far, m=main,
bg=background

COVER Jim Brandenburg/Minden Pictures/CO **BACK COVER** Audrey Snider-Bell/S
1 rattanapatphoto/S 2 Pedro Nogueira/S 3(bg) Curioso/S (strip, left to right) Villion
van Niekerk/S, Beverly Speed/S, Dennis Donohue/S, FloridaStock/S, S, 4–5 Design
Pics Inc/RF, 6–7(b) Eric Isselee/S, 6–7 (bg) Valentin Agapov/S, 6(bl) Clivia/F,
6(bl) ULKASTUDIO/S, 6(bl) Steve Bloom, 6(cr) ArtisticPhoto/S,
6(cr) Maslov Dmitry/S, 6(tl) Steffen Foerster/S, 7(bl) Edwin Giesbers/NPL,
7(br) Antoni Murcia/S, 7(cr) Daniel Cox/GI, 7(tl) Ljupco Smokovski/F, 7(tl) Nature
Production/NPL, 7(tl) RoyStudio.eu/S, 8–9 Jakub Krechowicz/S, 8–9 val lawless/S,
8–9(b) Noam Armonn/S, 8(b) Robert Valentic/NPL, 8(bg) Mark Yuill/S,
8(bl) SPbPhoto/S, 8(cb) gabor2100/S, 8(cr) Nadezhda Sundikova/S,
8(l) Oariff/D, 8(t) Picsfive/S, 8(t) oksankash/S, 9(b) Yganko/S, 9(bg) Mark Yuill/S,
9(br) Jabruson/NPL, 9(br) Carlos Horta/S, 9(br) Audrey Snider-Bell/S, 10(bl) MARTY
SNYDERMAN/VISUALS UNLIMITED, INC/SPL, 10(bl) Norbert Wu/Science Faction/CO,
10(tr) Design Pics Inc/RF, 11(b) Doug Perrine/NPL, 11(tl) EYE OF SCIENCE/SPL,
12–13 SteveUnit4/S, 12–13 zentilia/S, 12–13 Dr. Cloud/S, 12–13 Eky Studio/S,
12–13(b) Jag_cz/S, 12–13(bg) Fesus Robert/S, 12–13(bg) chaoss/S, 12(b) George
McCarthy/CO, 12(tr) Pete Oxford/Minden Pictures/FLPA, 13(b) Mark Moffett/Minden
Pictures/FLPA, 13(t) Lassi Rautiainen/NPL, 13(t) Dennis Donohue/S, 14–15 Potapov
Alexander/S, 14–15(bg) chalabala/S, 14(b) Massimo Saivezzo/S, 14(bl) NHPA/P,
14(tl) Potapov Alexander/S, 14(tr) Alex Hyde/NPL, 15(bl) Nick Upton/ NPL,
15(bl) Vitaly Korovin/S, 15(br) Daniel Heuclin/NPL, 15(t) Michael & Patricia
Fogden/GI, 16–17 Vividz Foto/S, 16–17 RTimages/S, 16–17(bg) khd/S,
16–17(bg) xpixel/S, 16(bc) Gary Blakeley/S, 16(cr) SJ Watt/S, 16(cr) Kevin
Schafer/Minden Pictures/FLPA, 16(cr) Angelo Gandolfi/NPL, 16(tl) RTimages/S,
17(br) Karsol/D, 17(br) Peter Betts/S, 17(cl) Clem Haagner/Ardea, 17(cl) Charidy
B/S, 17(cr) borzywoj/S, 17(tc) Florian Andronache/S, 18–19(bg) Kekyalyaynen/S,
18(b) Igor Kovalchuk/S, 18(bc) Alex Wild/Visuals Unlimited/CO, 18(bc) My Good
Images/S, 18(bl) Kerstin Schoene/S, 18(br) Kletr/S, 18(cl) SmileStudio/S,
18(tl) Andrey_Kuzmin/S, 18(tr) SCIEPRO/S, 19(bl) Dietmar Nill/NPL, 19(bl) Vitaly
Korovin/S, 19(cr) JAMES L. AMOS/NG, 19(t) Visuals Unlimited/CO, 20(bl) jps/S,
20(br) Raia/S, 20(br) Vitaly Korovin/S, 20(br) Westend61/SS, 20(tl) Kovalev
Maxim/S, 20(tr) Eric Isselee/S, 21(br) Raul D. Martin/ National Geographic
Society/CO, 21(br) Erik Stokker/S, 21(tr) Daniel Alvarez/S, 22(bl) Lions Gate/
Everett/RF, 22(cr) NHPA/P, 22(tl) Skymax/S, 22(tl) Ronnie Howard/S, 22(tr) Jean
Paul Ferrero/Ardea, 22(tr) Picsfive/S, 23(bl) Stephen Belcher/Minden Pictures/FLPA,

23(br) Myotis/S, 23(br) lenetstan/S, 23(br) Patryk Kosmider/S, 23(cl) Alhovik/S,
23(cl) Animals Animals/SS, 23(cr) Courtesy of Harvard University/Handout/
Reuters/CO, 23(cr) Luis Molinero/S, 23(tr) KONRAD WOTHE/ MINDEN PICTURES/NG,
23(tr) redsoul/S, 24–25 Picsfive/S, 24–25(b) Philip Perry/FLPA, 24–25(c) Ron
Austing/FLPA, 24(tr) Bernd Rohrschneider/FLPA, 25(b) Luiz Claudio Marigo/NPL,
25(tl) Nelson Marques/S, 25(tr) Stu Porter/S, 26 alexvav/S, 26–27 Nataliya Hora/S,
26–27(b) mradlgruber/S, 26–27(bg) Elenamiv/S, 26–27(c) Stefan Delle/S,
26–27(t) YKh/S, 26(bl) ROBERT SISSON/NG, 26(br) Nature Production/NPL,
26(tr) John Cancalosi/NPL, 27(br) Matty Symons/S, 27(l) Bob Jensen/P,
27(l) Collpicto/S, 27(tr) Ingo Arndt/NPL, 28–29 blojfo/S, 28–29(bg) Dirk Ercken/S,
28(bl) Jim Brandenburg/Minden Pictures/CO, 28(bl) Dima Fadeev/S, 28(bl) Yu
Lan/S, 28(cr) NHPA/P, 29(bl) JOEL SARTORE/NG, 29(cr) NHPA/P, 29(tl) DM7/S,
29(tl) R-studio/S, 30 Picsfive/S, 31 stock09/S, 31 val lawless/S, 31 AnnPainter/S,
30–31(c) CB2/ZOB/WENN.com/N, 30–31(t) Planner/S, 30(bl) Stephanie Frey/S,
30(bl) Steve Collender/S, 30(t) Picsfive/S, 30(tl) CB2/ZOB/WENN.com/N,
30(tr) Dr Shin-ya Ohba, 30(tr) R-studio/S, 30(tr) kanate/S, 31(b) Piyato/S,
31(bl) Faiz Zaki/S, 31(bl) Faiz Zaki/S, 31(cl) Earl D. Walker/S, 31(c) Korn/S,
31(r) CB2/ ZOB/WENN.com/N, 31(r) KROMKRATHOG/S, 32(cl) Tony Campbell/S,
32(tr) Michael & Patricia Fogden/Minden Pictures/FLPA, 33(b) LYNN M. STONE/NPL,
33(tl) Martin Zwick/NHPA/P, 33(tr) JONATHAN PLEDGER/S, 34–35(bg) Mrgreen/D,
34(bl) Doug Perrine/GI, 34(bl) Joe Gough/S, 34(bl) Oksana Nikolaieva/S,
34(bl) Alex Staroseltsev/S, 34(br) Winfried Wisniewski/GI, 34(br) Givaga/S,
34(cl) ivn3da/S, 34(cl) Nomad_Soul/S, 34(tl) Jaimie Duplass/S, 34(tl) Nixx
Photography/S, 34(tr) Anna Henly/GI, 34(tr) Kitch Bain/S, 34(tr) Oksana
Nikolaieva/S, 34(tr) Miro art studio/S, 35(bc) Vitaly Raduntsev/S,
35(bl) Lyutskevych Dar'ya/S, 35(bl) Minden Pictures/S, 35(cl) LHF Graphics/S,
35(cr) Julio Aldana/S, 35(cr) Nelia Sapronova/S, 35(t) Steven Kazlowski/Science
Faction/CO, 35(t) discpicture/S, 36–37 Tischenko Irina/S, 36(br) Suzi
Eszterhas/Minden Pictures/CO, 36(cl) Paul Souders/CO, 37(bc) Maridav/S,
37(br) Kathryn Jeffs/NPL, 37(cl) Doug Allan/NPL, 37(tr) Doug Allan/NPL,
38–39 moenez/S, 38–39 S, 38–39(bg) evv/S, 38(br) Loek Gerris/Foto
Natura/Minden Pictures/CO, 38(br) Milkovasa/S, 38(br) Elliotte Rusty Harold/S,
38(cr) imagebroker/A, 38(cr) tonyz20/S, 38(tl) ra2studio/S, 39(bl) cynoclub/S,
39(bl) age fotostock/SS, 39(c) Potapov Alexander/S, 39(cl) Handout/Reuters/CO,
39(tl) David & Debi Henshaw/S, 39(t) Sphinx Wang/S

All other photographs are from: Corel, digitalSTOCK, digitalvision, Dreamstime.com,
Fotolia.com, iStockphoto.com, John Foxx, PhotoAlto, PhotoDisc, PhotoEssentials,
PhotoPro, Stockbyte

Every effort has been made to acknowledge the source and copyright
holder of each picture. The publishers apologise for any unintentional
errors or omissions.

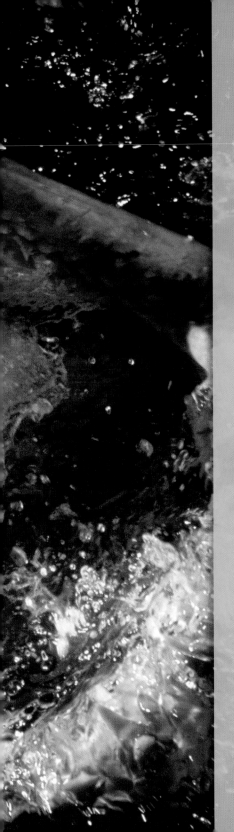

CONTENTS

◄ A great white shark's gaping mouth, lined with daggerlike teeth, looms menacingly upward, ready to engulf potential prey.

Family FEUDS

Family life in the animal world is not all fun and games. There is plenty of motivation for family fights—competition for food is a common source of friction. However, relatives do have their uses, especially when it comes to uniting against a common enemy.

BIRD BRAWL

Given their tendency for violence toward one another, it's a wonder that mallards are one of the most widespread duck species. Life for ducklings is unusually precarious because adults often attack and kill any youngsters they encounter—and some mothers have been known to kill their own offspring in cases of mistaken identity. Drakes (male mallards) also attack each other at breeding time in belligerent battles over territory and mating rights.

A drake may attempt to drown its rival by pinning it below the water.

In Botswana, two bull heads as they attempt to long tusks in a fight for can be so ferocious that

African elephants smash spear each other with their supremacy. Sometimes fights tusks break.

CLASH OF THE TITANS

Brotherly love counts for nothing in an elephant family when it is mating time. Females lead the herds, so when males reach adulthood they are expelled and forced to roam the African plains. Bulls (male elephants) have a reputation as loners, but they often travel with brothers, cousins, or best friends until they come into musth, and their hormones take over. Musth is a frenzied time of fighting when male aggression levels soar, and kinship is forgotten in a competition for mates. It's a conflict that frequently results in serious injury or even death.

A cuckoo chick ejects its host's chick—a reed warbler—out of the nest, leaving just one mouth to feed—its own!

CUCKOOS IN THE NEST

Bringing up youngsters is risky. For animals, the reward is that their genes are passed onto the next generation. However, sometimes nature plays cruel tricks with caring parents. Cuckoos are brood parasites and lay their eggs in the nests of smaller birds. When the cuckoo chicks hatch, they push the host bird's chicks and eggs out of the nest. Unaware, the host parents continue to raise the cuckoo, which even imitates the "hungry" call of the host's own chicks.

BRINGING UP BABY

There are few animals more dangerous than a mother bear. Once her maternal instincts have been aroused, an adult female with a cub to protect can turn from docile to deadly in seconds. Undaunted by the size of an attacker, mothers will use claws and jaws to fight to the death. They usually only give up when they believe the attacker is dead.

A young brown bear cub looks on as its mother fights off an aggressive male.

Male elephants that are successful in their fights may be able to find as many as 30 mates in just one year, and could father as many calves.

SCHOOL OF HARD KNOCKS

The speed and accuracy required for survival are skills that can take a long time to master, so many youngsters playfight almost as soon as they can walk. Rough and tumble is accompanied by mock punches and gentle bites as siblings develop their hunting and defense strategies.

Young fox cubs playfight with each other until they are around 16 weeks old.

HISSING Killers

There are around 3,000 species of snake, and among them are some of the world's deadliest animals. These scaly serpents are equipped with one of the most dangerous natural substances on Earth— venom. Those that live near human habitations cause many deaths. The Indian Cobra alone accounts for several thousand human fatalities every year.

▲ King cobras are the longest venomous snakes in the world, reaching 15 ft (4.6 m) in length.

Rapid elapids

Elapids are a family of snakes that are widespread, and their bite is often deadly to humans. All venomous snakes have fangs, but most elapids have hollow fangs, through which venom flows when the snake bites its victim. Most elapids are slender-bodied, fast movers—black mambas can slither faster than a human can run. A tiny amount of their venom—the weight of a banknote—is enough to kill 50 people.

Taipan terror

The Taipan, also known as the Fierce Snake, possesses one of the most deadly venoms in the world. It targets the nervous system, paralyzing breathing muscles. The snake devours its victim once it is dead. Taipans live in remote regions of Australia, and target lizards, rats, and other small mammals.

▲ This taipan is ready to strike— one drop of its venom is enough to kill 100 people.

LYSOL

Vicious vipers

Vipers have hollow fangs, which, at up to 2 in (5 cm) in length, are much longer than those of elapids. The fangs are hinged, folding away when not in use. Large glands attached to the fangs deliver a venom that attacks the victim's circulatory system, destroying body tissues and muscles. Vipers also have sensory pits on their heads that detect heat given off by prey, allowing them to hunt effectively under the cover of darkness.

ABOUT 600 SNAKE SPECIES ARE VENOMOUS. FEWER THAN ONE THIRD ARE DANGEROUS TO HUMANS.

SQUEEZED TO DEATH

Boas and pythons—constrictors—do not use venom to kill their prey. Instead, they rely on stealth, and their huge size and strength. They can easily kill animals larger than themselves. The secret to their success lies in a constrictor's ability to grip and squeeze. Once it has caught an animal, the snake wraps its muscular coils around it. Each time its victim breathes out, the snake squeezes a little tighter, until the prey finally suffocates.

▼ A python will check each meal's size and shape before working its extending mouth over one end.

PERFECT
Predator

Sharks are awesome hunters of the world's oceans. They have evolved over more then 450 million years to become near-perfect predators. This animal's armory includes: a streamlined body packed with fast-acting muscles, powerful jaws full of razor-sharp teeth, enamel-plated skin, and acute senses.

DETECTION DEVICES

Sharks' extraordinary senses help to make them exceptional hunters. The lateral line, which runs along the length of their body, is made up of sensitive pores that detect any movement in the water. Sharks have large eyeballs, which see partially in color, and some species are able to see well in the dark. Around the mouth, sensory cells are focused in pits called ampullae of Lorenzini. These pits sense the electricity emitted by the muscles of animals nearby.

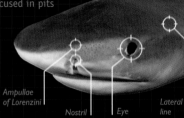

Ampullae of Lorenzini
Nostril   *Eye*   *Lateral line*

A shark uses a variety of senses to pick up information about its environment, both near and far.

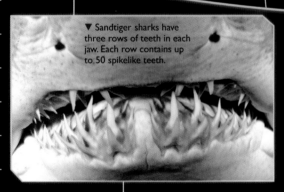

▼ Sandtiger sharks have three rows of teeth in each jaw. Each row contains up to 50 spikelike teeth.

TOOLS FOR THE JOB

A shark's teeth are a guide to its diet. Long, slender, ultrasharp teeth are perfect for gripping slippery squid. Triangular, multi-cusped teeth that look like a saw edge are for carving through flesh and bone. Rows of small, sharp teeth are ideal for grabbing prey from the seabed, and broad, platelike ones can crush the shells of sea turtles.

COOKIE MONSTER

Cookiecutter sharks may be relatively small at just 20 in (50 cm) in length, but they are one of the most savage shark species. A cookiecutter approaches its prey with stealth and speed, then clamps onto its body with its suckerlike mouth, sinking in its rows of sharp teeth. The shark twists its body, making a circular cut, and tears a golf ball-sized plug of flesh away.

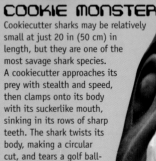

▶ The teeth in a cookiecutter's lower jaw are all joined together and look like the edge of a saw.

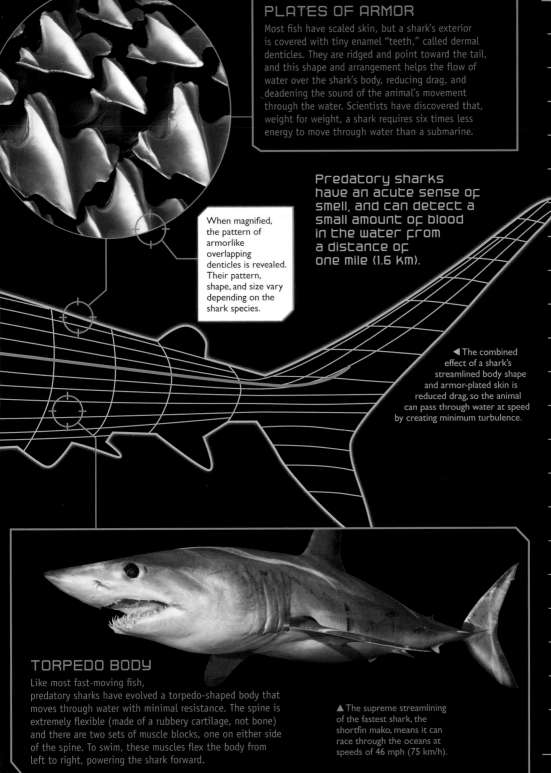

PLATES OF ARMOR

Most fish have scaled skin, but a shark's exterior is covered with tiny enamel "teeth," called dermal denticles. They are ridged and point toward the tail, and this shape and arrangement helps the flow of water over the shark's body, reducing drag, and deadening the sound of the animal's movement through the water. Scientists have discovered that, weight for weight, a shark requires six times less energy to move through water than a submarine.

Predatory sharks have an acute sense of smell, and can detect a small amount of blood in the water from a distance of one mile (1.6 km).

When magnified, the pattern of armorlike overlapping denticles is revealed. Their pattern, shape, and size vary depending on the shark species.

◀ The combined effect of a shark's streamlined body shape and armor-plated skin is reduced drag, so the animal can pass through water at speed by creating minimum turbulence.

TORPEDO BODY

Like most fast-moving fish, predatory sharks have evolved a torpedo-shaped body that moves through water with minimal resistance. The spine is extremely flexible (made of a rubbery cartilage, not bone) and there are two sets of muscle blocks, one on either side of the spine. To swim, these muscles flex the body from left to right, powering the shark forward.

▲ The supreme streamlining of the fastest shark, the shortfin mako, means it can race through the oceans at speeds of 46 mph (75 km/h).

FIGHT-OFF

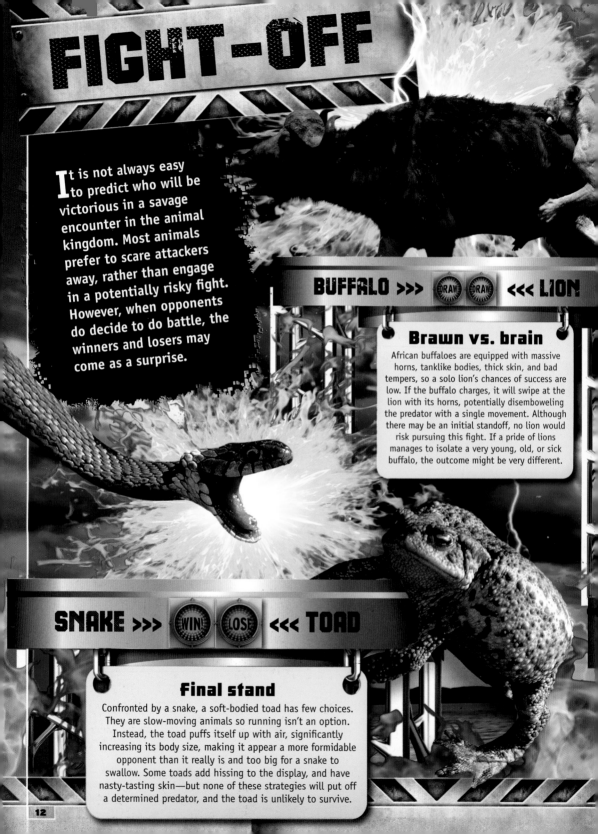

It is not always easy to predict who will be victorious in a savage encounter in the animal kingdom. Most animals prefer to scare attackers away, rather than engage in a potentially risky fight. However, when opponents do decide to do battle, the winners and losers may come as a surprise.

BUFFALO >>> DRAW DRAW <<< LION

Brawn vs. brain

African buffaloes are equipped with massive horns, tanklike bodies, thick skin, and bad tempers, so a solo lion's chances of success are low. If the buffalo charges, it will swipe at the lion with its horns, potentially disemboweling the predator with a single movement. Although there may be an initial standoff, no lion would risk pursuing this fight. If a pride of lions manages to isolate a very young, old, or sick buffalo, the outcome might be very different.

SNAKE >>> WIN! LOSE <<< TOAD

Final stand

Confronted by a snake, a soft-bodied toad has few choices. They are slow-moving animals so running isn't an option. Instead, the toad puffs itself up with air, significantly increasing its body size, making it appear a more formidable opponent than it really is and too big for a snake to swallow. Some toads add hissing to the display, and have nasty-tasting skin—but none of these strategies will put off a determined predator, and the toad is unlikely to survive.

BEAR >>> DRAW DRAW **<<< WOLF**

Dead heat

Wolves are pack hunters that employ sophisticated hunting techniques, while bears mostly rely on a diet of roots, fruits, and berries. Wolves and bears do not normally prey on one another, but they are territorial and protective of their young—traits that can lead to deadly standoffs. Both contenders possess speed, brains, power, and massive jaws. However, although the animals will snarl and bare their teeth for intimidation, the confrontation will end in a draw. Combat would prove too costly for either party, and a face-saving withdrawal is the only sensible option.

SPIDER >>> LOSE WIN **<<< WASP**

Spider snacks

Giant tarantula hawk wasps grow as long as a finger, and have powerful stings 0.25 in (6 mm) long. The wasp attacks its tarantula prey by grabbing one of its legs, and, undeterred by the flurry of irritating hairs that the spider hurls, stings its underside. The wasp drags its paralyzed victim into its burrow and lays an egg in its flesh. The newly hatched larva will feast on the still-living spider.

THE VENOMOUS STING OF A TARANTULA HAWK WASP IS EXCRUCIATING AND CAN CAUSE PERMANENT NERVE DAMAGE IN HUMANS.

ARACHNID Assassins

Arachnids are some of the most successful hunters in the world. Eight nimble legs allow them to leap into action instantly, often seizing their prey before their presence has even been detected. Spiders are arachnids that produce silk—a strong, stretchy thread, perfect for trapping prey—and venom. Fierce-looking scorpions kill with a stabbing stinger.

▼ A net-casting spider holds its web stretched between its legs, ready to snatch any unsuspecting victim below.

Webs, nets, and traps

Orb spiders build typical disk-shaped webs and wait for prey to approach, but net-casting spiders take their web to their prey. Net-casting spiders first spin a small web net. Then, holding it stretched taut between their extra-long front limbs, they leap onto their prey, trapping and wrapping it in silk. Also known as ogre-faced spiders, two of these arachnids' eight eyes are enormous, giving them exceptional night vision.

LETHAL DOSE

Sydney funnelweb spiders combine aggression with powerful venom, making them one of the most dangerous spiders for humans to encounter. They are often found in and around houses and outbuildings in the area around Sydney, Australia. People used to die from the Sydney funnelweb's bite, but since an antivenom was produced in the 1980s, far fewer people have been affected.

◀ The Sydney funnelweb uses its two sharp fangs to strike hard and deliver its potentially lethal dose of venom.

Desert demon

Solifugids may not have stings or venom, but they are fearsome hunters. Their giant fanged, pincerlike mouthparts are the key to their success. These desert-living arachnids usually lurk in cool burrows, or hang from branches during the day. At night, they leave the safety of their dens and go on the rampage, killing large numbers of bugs and spiders, and even larger prey such as rodents and lizards. Their mouthparts can cut through skin and thin bone, dicing a victim's body to pieces in minutes.

◀ A solifugid looks rather like an alien with its bristled face, massive jaws, and beady black eyes.

> SOLIFUGIDS DART TOWARD PREY IN THE BLINK OF AN EYE—THEY CAN RUN 20 IN (50 CM) PER SECOND.

▼ A goldenrod crab spider sinks its fangs into an unsuspecting horsefly.

Crab soup

Crab spiders don't use webs to catch prey. Instead, they lie in wait, expertly camouflaged in their surroundings, to ambush bugs. Some resemble bark, leaves, or bird droppings, while others are brightly colored to match flower petals. A crab spider's venom is strong enough to kill insects bigger than itself. Once a bug has been disabled by a venomous bite, a crab spider will vomit digestive juices onto the victim, so that its tissues dissolve. Then the spider can consume its victim as a "soup."

Sting in the tail

The deathstalker scorpion has a reputation as one of the most dangerous on Earth, even though it is only 3–4 in (7–10 cm) in length. Its claws are small and feeble, but this means it is quick to strike with a sting-bearing tail. The venom is extremely powerful, even in small quantities, and quickly paralyzes a potential meal, or an attacker. To a healthy adult human a deathstalker sting is excruciatingly painful, but its consequences can be far more deadly for a child.

◀ A deathstalker's pincerlike pedipalps (claws) are used to grab prey.

ANGRY Birds

Not all birds sit on branches and sing sweetly while eyeing up a juicy berry to eat. Some are born hunters, with weapons to match their savage instincts. Owls and raptors—birds of prey—are notorious, but there are also some unexpected killers in the bird kingdom.

DIVE BOMBER

CLAWED KICKER

Golden eagle
(Aquila chrysaetos)

With a colossal wingspan of up to 7.5 ft (2.3 m) and a top speed of 150 mph (240 km/h), a golden eagle in pursuit of prey is a force to be reckoned with. These raptors dive-bomb their prey, directing a death-blow to the back of the neck. Unlike most raptors, golden eagles often select quarry that are bigger than themselves. The bulk of their diet is made up of small animals such as rabbits and reptiles, but they also attack deer and livestock, including cattle.

Southern cassowary
(Casuarius casuarius)

Cassowaries are large, flightless birds that live in the forests of New Guinea and northeast Australia. They have muscular legs that pack a powerful kick, and, with a 4-in- (10-cm-) long claw on the inside toe of each foot, can inflict a nasty puncture wound. These birds are not hunters, and normally only attack humans to defend themselves or their eggs. They communicate with deep booming calls that are just within the range of human hearing.

Red-backed shrike
(Lanius collurio)

Insect-eating butcherbirds and shrikes have an impressive way to store their food. Once they have caught a small animal or bug, they dispatch it with a vicious peck, and then impale it on a thorn, or barbed wire. This creates a larder that may contain several bugs, small mammals, and reptiles. This gory store of food sustains the birds when they fail to catch anything, and it also impresses potential mates.

BUTCHER BIRD

Secretary bird
(Sagittarius serpentarius)

Long legs help the secretary bird march through the tall grass of the African savanna, stalking prey. These large, slender birds stamp on grass to flush out big insects, small mammals, and snakes to eat. They deliver immense kicks to any animals that bolt, and protect themselves from potentially venomous snake bites by spreading their wings and using them as shields. They can cover more than 19 mi (31 km) in a single day of hunting.

SPEED DEMON

STALKING STAMPER

Ostrich
(Struthio camelus)

Male ostriches usually reserve their aggression for other males, and are swift to attack during the breeding season. They are famous for their bad tempers, so humans and even vehicles are often the focus of ostrich assaults! The tallest, heaviest, and fastest of all birds, the ostrich can reach speeds of more than 43 mph (70 km/h)—and can keep running for an hour or more.

BLOOD
Suckers

Animals that feed on blood have a highly specialized way of life, and are usually parasites. Bloodsuckers have a range of ways to pierce skin to get at the protein-packed, nutritious red liquid. Known as hematophagy, feeding on blood is not confined to mosquitoes and vampire bats—some species of bird, fish, moth, and other bugs also enjoy a bloody feast.

SUPPLY PROBLEMS

A TICK FEEDING ON AN ANIMAL VICTIM

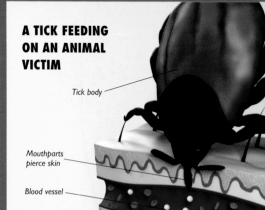

Tick body

Mouthparts pierce skin

Blood vessel

Blood is a wholesome meal, but bloodsucking animals have to be able to find a source, then access it —usually by penetrating scales, feathers, or skin. Techniques for finding a blood source include hearing movement, sensing body heat, following the trail of carbon dioxide breathed out by potential victims, and detecting pheromones (chemicals released by animals). Accessing the blood source normally involves specialized mouthparts that can pierce the host's skin and break into blood vessels, or scrape away at the flesh to create a bleeding wound.

Hungry mothers

Female mosquitoes must feed on the protein and iron found in blood before they can lay eggs. The fly's syringelike mouthpart—a proboscis—pierces skin and delivers anticoagulants as blood is sucked up, to stop clotting. Each mosquito takes a tiny amount of blood, but the damage to the victim lies in the deadly microorganisms that these bugs often leave behind. Mosquitoes can transmit diseases such as malaria, dengue fever, yellow fever, and encephalitis.

▶ Worldwide research continues into the problem of deadly diseases that are transmitted by mosquitoes.

Sucker fish

Sea lampreys are parasitic jawless fish that mostly feed on other fish and marine mammals. They attach to their victims with suckerlike mouths lined with rows of horny teeth that scrape away at the flesh. As they feed, lampreys douse the wound with anticoagulants. Once its stomach is full, the lamprey disengages its mouth from the victim and falls away, leaving a gaping, bleeding wound.

▶ Lampreys become parasites when they are adults, and use their circular, toothed mouths to latch onto fish, such as trout (inset). They feed until they are ready to mate and die after their eggs are laid.

DRACULA BATS

Vampire bats have powerful hind legs and unusually strong thumbs that help them crawl and clamber onto a victim.

Vampires really do exist, but these bats scarcely deserve the gruesome reputation they have acquired since the first stories of Dracula. Most species of vampire bat feed on the blood of cows and horses, not humans. Vampire bats need to consume about two tablespoons of blood a day—more than half of their body weight. They have pit organs on their faces that are covered with heat-detecting molecules to sense body heat. Furtive vampire bats crawl on the ground to approach their prey, and sink their ultrasharp fangs into a spot where blood is close to the surface. They produce a chemical that reduces pain, and keeps the blood flowing as they lap.

TEETH and JaWS

MAXIMUM ANIMAL BITE FORCES
Figures are estimates, shown in Newtons (N)

Carcharodon megalodon (extinct giant shark)	182,200 N
Tyrannosaurus rex	60,000 N
Great white shark	17,790 N
Saltwater crocodile	16,460 N
Dunkleosteus terrelli (extinct marine fish)	5,000 N
African lion	4,500 N
Hyena	2,000 N
Human	890 N
Tasmanian devil	553 N

About 430 to 445 million years ago the first jawed animals evolved. Their jaws developed from gill arches—the bony parts that support a fish's gill slits. Jaws allowed fish to become hunters rather than just being passive eaters. Today, predators show a range of highly specialized jaws and teeth that can grab, squash, pierce, grind, slice, slash, and mash.

▼ *Dunkleosteus* lived about 360 million years ago.

▼ A lioness in Botswana uses her carnassial teeth to shear flesh from a buffalo carcass.

JAWS OF THE DEEP
The prehistoric seas were home to *Dunkleosteus*, a giant sharklike fish with bizarre structures for biting. Instead of teeth, *Dunkleosteus* had large bony blades in its jaws, which could slice effectively. They were capable of crushing bone—*Dunkleosteus* had the second strongest bite of any fish—and turning fish prey into mincemeat in minutes. This marine monster was protected from attack by an armor-plated skull.

Carnivore club
Meat-eating predators, such as lions, have skulls packed with large muscles and outsize teeth. This allows the jaw to exert a massive bite force with incredible grip. The upper and lower jaw are connected by a hinge joint that allows movement vertically only. Supersized temporalis muscles that operate the jaws are so large that they make up most of the bulk of a lion's head. Carnivore canine teeth are enlarged, sharp, and pointed for piercing flesh, while scissorlike carnassial teeth that line the sides of the jaws shred and shear flesh.

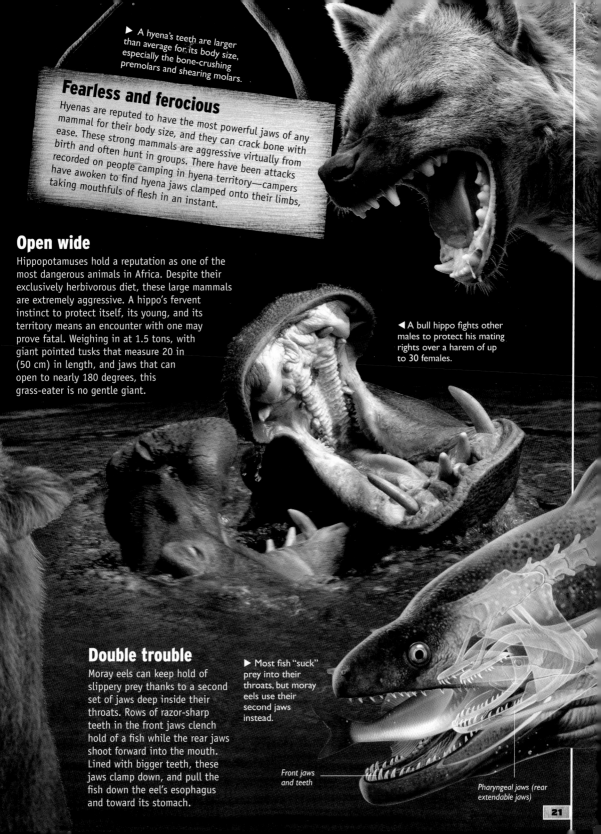

► A hyena's teeth are larger than average for its body size, especially the bone-crushing premolars and shearing molars.

Fearless and ferocious

Hyenas are reputed to have the most powerful jaws of any mammal for their body size, and they can crack bone with ease. These strong mammals are aggressive virtually from birth and often hunt in groups. There have been attacks recorded on people camping in hyena territory—campers have awoken to find hyena jaws clamped onto their limbs, taking mouthfuls of flesh in an instant.

Open wide

Hippopotamuses hold a reputation as one of the most dangerous animals in Africa. Despite their exclusively herbivorous diet, these large mammals are extremely aggressive. A hippo's fervent instinct to protect itself, its young, and its territory means an encounter with one may prove fatal. Weighing in at 1.5 tons, with giant pointed tusks that measure 20 in (50 cm) in length, and jaws that can open to nearly 180 degrees, this grass-eater is no gentle giant.

◄ A bull hippo fights other males to protect his mating rights over a harem of up to 30 females.

Double trouble

Moray eels can keep hold of slippery prey thanks to a second set of jaws deep inside their throats. Rows of razor-sharp teeth in the front jaws clench hold of a fish while the rear jaws shoot forward into the mouth. Lined with bigger teeth, these jaws clamp down, and pull the fish down the eel's esophagus and toward its stomach.

► Most fish "suck" prey into their throats, but moray eels use their second jaws instead.

Front jaws and teeth

Pharyngeal jaws (rear extendable jaws)

PAWS and Claws

Powerful paws and lacerating claws are key weapons, allowing an animal to inflict injury while keeping its own head out of the line of fire. Clawed paws are often specialized, with features that have evolved to match the hunting requirements of their owner.

SPURS OF VENOM

The duck-billed platypus is one of very few types of venomous mammal in the world. Only males possess a curved claw, or spur, on each of their hind legs. These spurs are attached to glands that release venom. Males only use their spurs when kicking out at their natural enemies and other males, especially at mating time.

▲ A platypus's venom is not deadly to humans, but it is said to cause intense pain.

◀ A polar bear's huge paws can be up to 12 in (30 cm) in diameter.

Polar paws

Polar bears are the largest carnivores on land, and they have huge paws to match. In their Arctic habitat, broad paws act like snowshoes, spreading the polar bear's weight on snow and thin ice. They also help the bears to stalk their seal prey—tufts of fur between the toes deaden the noise of their step. Short, stout, curved claws pierce and rip flesh easily, and can haul a seal out of an ice hole to eat.

Indian devils

Wolverines may be no bigger than dogs, but these fearless creatures attack bears and deer, earning them the alternative name of "Indian devil." They are weasel-like mammals that live in northern regions where polar conditions leave predators hungry, desperate, and fearless. A wolverine's paws are large, flat, and furry with broad pads and very long claws. They are perfect for chasing down prey over deep snow, and holding onto a victim while the wolverine delivers a neck-breaking bite with its immensely powerful jaws.

▶ Wolverines both hunt and scavenge, feasting on any animal they can find.

▲ At rest, the hairy frog doesn't look special, but its hidden weapon makes potential attackers think twice.

Snap claws

In the natural world, fact can be stranger than fiction. When threatened, African hairy frogs snap the bones in their feet. The broken bones rip through the skin, jutting out as knifelike extensions on the the frog's fingertips and toes. This gives them an effective set of razor-sharp claws to swipe at an attacker.

Crushing coconuts

When Charles Darwin encountered the world's largest land-living species of crab on the Keeling Islands, he described it as "monstrous." These land-living crustaceans, which are known as robber or coconut crabs, have a legspan of up to 40 in (one meter). Coconut crabs feed mainly on fruit, and their name comes from their ability to open the tough shells of coconuts. Occasionally they use their enormous claws to attack other crabs, and they have been known to turn cannibal and eat their fallen opponent after a fight.

▲ A coconut crab's strong claws can easily pull its body up a tree to reach the fruit at the top.

CRABS HAVE ONE OF THE GREATEST CLAW FORCES FOR BODY SIZE IN THE ANIMAL KINGDOM.

Feline FIENDS

Cats are famous for their killing skills—their supreme strength and elegance combine to create a sublime predator. Cats all share the same basic body features. They have short muzzles equipped with wide-opening jaws, sharp fangs, and meat-shearing carnassial teeth. They also all have highly developed senses, powerful limbs, and paws that are tooled with retractable claws.

◀ A lioness keeps low to the ground as she stalks prey at dusk.

STEALTH

1

Few animals can stalk their prey with the stealth of a cat. Colored or patterned fur helps a cat to remain hidden in undergrowth as it chooses and follows a potential victim. A characteristic crawl, with its body close to the ground, allows the predator to creep closer—its unblinking eyes fixed and focused on the prey. Leopards move so quietly that they have been known to pluck a sleeping human victim from their bed and escape without a sound—the room's other occupants only find out about the midnight visitor the next morning.

SPEED

2

Felines are able to accelerate fast but, unlike members of the dog family, are unable to sustain a chase for long. Cheetahs are the swiftest of all land animals over short distances. A very narrow body, slender limb bones, almost vertical shoulder blades, and a flexible spine mean this cat is not just streamlined, it can make enormous energy-efficient strides. However, at high speeds the cat gets so hot that it cannot run further than about 1,600 ft (500 m) during a chase before risking death from overheating.

POUNCE

▶ A caracal's long, strong back legs are perfect for running down speedy prey such as hares and antelopes.

ONE FEARLESS LEOPARD IN INDIA WAS PROBABLY RESPONSIBLE FOR MORE THAN 125 HUMAN DEATHS IN JUST TEN YEARS.

THE FEAR FACTOR

When an animal knows a big cat is nearby, the fear factor takes over. Their body goes into a state of stress, ready to run or defend itself—the "fight or flight" response. Adrenaline courses through the blood vessels, increasing the rate of blood circulation, breathing, metabolism of carbohydrates, and preparing the muscles for exertion. Although felines are superb predators, most of their potential victims escape unharmed.

▲ A gazelle bounds away from its hunter —the big cat.

◄ Mid-chase, a cheetah lowers its head for extra streamlining, and extends its claws for a better grip on the ground.

Leaping and pouncing skills give a feline the advantage of surprise. Prey may have judged their stalker to be at a safe distance, only to be shocked, seconds later, to find a fanged set of jaws looming overhead. Snow leopards hold the record for the longest recorded leap of any cat, at 49 ft (15 m), but caracals and servals are the bounciest cats. Pouncing enables a cat to approach its prey from above, which means it can avoid potential bites and scratches while delivering a lethal blow.

3

In the final stages of a hunt, cats employ speed and strength and go for the throat. With their jaws tightly clamped around the windpipe, a cat effectively suffocates its prey, and the victim usually suffers a quick death. Large cats can hunt prey bigger than themselves, and often drag their victim to a safe location before settling down to eat.

▼ A jaguar clamps its strong jaws onto the skull of an unfortunate caiman.

4

SLAUGHTER

BRUTAL
Bugs

▶ A tailless whip scorpion begins to munch through the body of a grasshopper.

You don't have to be big to be brutal. Skulking beneath rocks, lurking in the undergrowth, flitting through the air, and even hiding in our homes there is an almost invisible world of mini-monsters, battling it out for survival.

Acid attack

Giant vinegaroons resemble a cross between a scorpion and a spider, and share some of the most savage characteristics of both. These arachnids—also known as whip scorpions—grab their invertebrate victims with their heavy, armored pedipalps and crush them to death. They deter predators by bombarding them with a noxious spray that is 84 percent acid.

▼ Bulldog ants are only found in Australia. They live in colonies but forage and hunt alone—mostly feeding on smaller carpenter ants.

▶ Capable of killing 40 honeybees in a minute, this giant hornet kills more people in Japan every year than any other animal.

Nonstop stingers

Ants are brutal bugs with vicious stings—they belong to the same family as bees, wasps, and hornets. Bullet ants are named for their stings, which are said to feel like a gunshot, and fire ants hold tight to an attacker and keep stinging for as long as they can. Bulldog ants are fierce, but one look at their menacing jaws should be enough to scare any attacker away.

Big, bold, and bad

In Japan, Asian giant hornets are called sparrow-wasps because at 2 in (5 cm) in length, they look similar to small birds when in flight. Like other members of the bee and wasp family, these insects administer pain-inducing stings, but they also inject a neurotoxin that can prove lethal. Thankfully they usually reserve their aggression for colonies of honeybees rather than people.

▶ The moon moth caterpillar uses both camouflage and toxic spines to defend itself.

Death by caterpillar

It is hard to believe that soft-bodied, plant-eating caterpillars could inflict a potentially fatal wound on any creature, yet some caterpillars have been known to kill humans. Lonomia caterpillars gather together in large groups, on the ground, or in trees. They are covered in detachable hairy spines that deliver powerful chemicals that burn, and cause swelling, headaches, and blisters. Within 12 hours the worst possible symptom may occur—the victim slowly bleeds to death.

Creepy-crawly killer

People living in the southwestern region of the United States fear the giant centipede *Scolopendra heros*, with good reason. These invertebrates can grow to 8 in (20 cm) in length and inflict an incredibly painful bite, thanks to the venom that all centipedes possess. Larger centipedes can deliver more venom with each bite, so the Amazonian giant centipede—which grows to 12 in (30 cm) long—is best avoided.

◀ Giant centipedes mostly hunt other invertebrates, such as beetles and flies, but they also feed on birds, mice, lizards, and frogs.

Cold-blooded
KILLERS

Most reptiles and amphibians are active hunters. These are ancient groups of animals that have developed a diverse range of hunting techniques. There are cannibalistic "dragons," sit-and-wait predators, stalking crocodilians, slimy salamanders, and even frogs with fangs.

CAUTION: Surinam horned frog

Surinam horned frogs are expert ambushers. Their peculiar flattened appearance allows these large amphibians to partly bury themselves in the ground and remain undetected by prey. When victims approach, the frogs leap into action. Unusually for frogs, they have toothlike bony projections from the jaw, so they immobilize their prey with a single bite before swallowing it whole.

▶ A Surinam horned frog may sit absolutely still for several days, waiting for lunch—such as a bullfrog—to pass by.

DANGER: Nile crocodile

Many savage animals only resort to aggression when provoked, or in self-defense. However, crocodiles almost always attack with a single purpose in mind—getting a meal. Most crocodiles ambush their prey, and typically attack at the water's edge. They lunge forward, take a strong hold with their jaws, and pull the victim underwater. Once there, they will roll around in the water, which can disorientate prey, drown it, and snap its spine.

◀ A crocodile's eyes, ears, and nose are all on top of its head, so that it can lie in wait for prey almost completely submerged.

THE KILLER QUESTION

A mystery surrounds the savage lifestyle of *Tyrannosaurus rex*. While this dinosaur certainly had the appearance of a ferocious predator, scientists argue that it may have been more of a scavenger. They argue that its hind limbs would have been far too heavy for fast running, and that those feeble forearms would not have been much use in grabbing prey. It has also been suggested that *T rex* was a cannibal and had lethal bacteria in its saliva, like the Komodo dragon of today.

WARNING: Komodo dragon

The Lesser Sunda Islands in Indonesia are so remote that the existence of their now most famous inhabitants was widely unknown until 100 years ago. Komodo dragons are the largest living lizards, reaching 10 ft (3 m) in length. They combine a monstrous appearance with a savage nature—feeding on almost anything, and attacking large animals, including humans. Adult Komodos will also eat younger members of their own species, so youngsters often have to hide in trees to avoid being eaten.

▼ An antelope's leg disappears down a dragon's gaping throat—an adult Komodo can eat up to 80 percent of its own body weight at one time.

HAZARD: Japanese giant salamander

Salamanders are amphibians, like frogs and toads, but with tails. They are all carnivores, but they can withstand long periods without any food at all. Many are dull-colored for camouflage but fire salamanders have bold yellow markings to warn that they produce a toxic substance. Japanese giant salamanders grow to almost 5 ft (1.5 m). They have slimy, mucus-covered skin and huge mouths. They lie in wait for food to pass by and grab prey with an almighty snap of their jaws.

◄ At night a Japanese giant salamander is alert, but in the day it rests beneath rocks.

RIVER SAFARI

Under the still surface of a lake or the gently rippling waters of a river, undiscovered assassins lurk. Although humans have been using waterways for many thousands of years, the waters still hide many savage secrets. We are only just beginning to understand what an incredible wealth of fascinating animal stories the world's rivers have to tell.

Mystery monster

Giant freshwater stingrays are among the world's biggest river killers. At half the length of a bus, they are strong enough to pull boats along rivers or underwater. Giant stingrays remained undiscovered until the 1990s and new species are now being identified in Indo-Pacific river regions. Stingrays are usually passive fish, but they may attack people who try to handle them. Their tails have arrowlike barbs of up to 15 in (38 cm) that can break through skin and penetrate bone to deliver deadly venom.

▶ Despite their awesome size, giant stingrays are difficult to find, catch, or study.

Big, bad bugs

Giant water bugs are the largest insect river monsters in the world. They can walk, fly, and swim, using their wings to store air while they hunt underwater. These huge aquatic insects sit motionless waiting for prey to approach them, then make a grab with pincerlike front legs. Needlelike mouthparts inject saliva into the victim, and its body juices are sucked out.

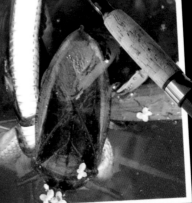

Water bugs have been observed eating baby turtles, and even snakes.

Man-eating catfish

Tales of man-eating catfish have been around for centuries, and the wels catfish is often named as the number one suspect. These massive fish are certainly equipped to kill, with huge jaws lined with hundreds of small teeth and an aggressive temperament at mating time. While this fish may pose some risk to humans, its natural prey are much smaller— crustaceans, fish, frogs, worms, and ducks.

▶ Little is known about these monster fish, so explorer Zeb Hogan has launched a project to protect them and other freshwater giants.

Survival strategy

The alligator gar is a menacing megafish with a long, toothed snout. It preys on fish, turtles, and birds. The gar's eggs and yolk sacs have a very unusual feature that has doubtless helped these ancient fish to survive—they are toxic to crustaceans and many vertebrates. Crayfish and blue crabs are especially vulnerable to the poison, and even humans are affected just by handling alligator gar eggs.

▶ An alligator gar can grow to 10 ft (3 m) in length and gets its name from its long, toothy snout.

WIGGLING, WRIGGLING WORMS

A primitive beast lurks in the murky waters of swamps in the southeastern states of the U.S.—the alligator snapping turtle. This ancient animal demonstrates an impressive hunting trick—it lies with its jaws wide open to expose a red wriggling structure on its tongue, which looks like a worm. Fish are tempted into the monster's beaklike mouth, which then slams shut.

Wels catfish use their barbels (whiskerlike sense organs) to taste, and feel their way in murky water.

With its dull colors and strange body shape, an alligator snapping turtle has perfect camouflage.

SMASH! BANG! WALLOP!

Gripping jaws, **snipping** teeth, gripping claws—for some animals these standard tools of **savagery** are far too predictable. They use rather more surprising techniques to overpower their enemies, and get their point across in style.

Male strawberry poison frogs prefer to wrestle in the mornings. In the afternoon they eat, mate, and look after their young.

Two whitetail deer bucks square up for battle. Extra-thick skulls help protect their brains from the damaging effects of a smashing time.

CRUNCH!

GRAPPLE!

For a male antelope or deer, the rewards for fighting are high and the winner takes it all.

These animals operate harems, which means one male can win mating rights over a whole group of females, ensuring that future generations will carry his genes. In some species of antelope, horns can grow to 5 ft (1.5 m) in length—and particularly impressive horns may help a male to assert his dominance over other males without the need for fighting. However, if a fight-off is necessary, the stakes are high. Broken horns are a common injury following head-butting clashes, but others can be far more life-threatening.

Male strawberry poison frogs are proud homeowners, but they only welcome guests of the female kind. A male spends the morning warning neighboring males to keep their distance, but if one does stray over the invisible boundary a flesh-on-flesh battle will follow. The males hold tight and wrestle to the ground, pushing one another with their strong legs—the loser is forced to the ground and must leave the area in shame.

POISON FROGS HAVE FEW ENEMIES, AS THEIR COLORFUL SKIN IS HIGHLY TOXIC.

PUNCH!

Male Eastern gray kangaroos fight at mating time, but these sparring skills are also useful for battling dingos (wild dogs).

Kangaroos are famous for their kickboxing skills. These marsupial bruisers put everything into a confrontation—jabbing with clawed forepaws, grappling, and delivering mighty kicks from muscular hindlegs.

Hooved animals can use brute force to demolish any opposition. A fast kick delivers bone-crunching force, which is why horses and zebras are animals to be respected. Zebra stallions fight over mating rights and feeding grounds. In the first instance a small kick may be enough to persuade rivals to move, but if that doesn't work a stallion may deliver a series of deadly blows, usually aimed at a rival's head.

THWACK!

It takes great strength and agility for a zebra to launch an attack, but for the victor this vicious battle will be worth the effort.

NIP!

When males of almost any species square up to each other, there is a show of size and strength. Male swans raise their bodies out of the water, spread their wings and curve their necks—and the smaller bird may turn tail at this point. If not, a vicious battle may follow and can result in death. Wings and beaks are used as weapons.

The strongest swan sends its male rival packing with a wallop of the wings and a few sharp nips with a powerful beak.

COOL, CRUEL World

Life in the extreme habitats of the Arctic and Antarctic poses particular problems for wildlife. Without warmth and light to support much plant growth on land, most of the animals that survive here have to be meat or fish eaters. The outcome of a hunt may spell life or death when the next meal may be many miles, or days, away.

White wanderer

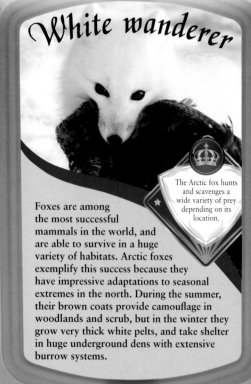

Foxes are among the most successful mammals in the world, and are able to survive in a huge variety of habitats. Arctic foxes exemplify this success because they have impressive adaptations to seasonal extremes in the north. During the summer, their brown coats provide camouflage in woodlands and scrub, but in the winter they grow very thick white pelts, and take shelter in huge underground dens with extensive burrow systems.

The Arctic fox hunts and scavenges a wide variety of prey depending on its location.

A parasitic copepod is just visible, attached to this Greenland shark's eye.

Ice shark

Ancient, slow-moving assassins live beneath the Arctic ice. Greenland sharks are the second-largest carnivorous sharks in the world. They only grow 0.5 in (one centimeter) per year, so a 20 ft (6 m) individual may be centuries old. Young Greenland sharks are likely to prey upon seals. Older individuals often have to scavenge, after parasites attack their eyes, making them blind.

AVIAN THUG

Arctic skuas have a huge range, and spend their summers along northern coasts of America and Europe. They are also known as parasitic jaegers.

Arctic skuas are kleptoparasites (food thieves), predators, and scavengers. One tactic is to threaten other birds until they regurgitate food, which the skua then eats. They attack smaller birds, and even dive-bomb large animals, including humans. Most onslaughts are aerial attacks, but some skuas have been seen sneaking up on nesting colonies of Arctic terns on foot. This approach fools the terns, which did not notice their eggs and chicks being stolen until too late.

ARCTIC ASSASSIN

Polar bears are the biggest and most ruthless of all bears. Their immense bodies are packed with muscles and fat, and they require an energy-rich diet to keep warm, and to power their predatory lifestyles. One bear needs to kill up to 75 seals per year to survive, but can live for up to eight months without feeding. Polar bears are one of the few predators that are known to hunt humans actively for food, although females are most dangerous when they are protecting their cubs.

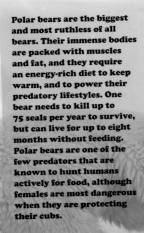

Polar bear mothers teach their cubs to hunt. These cubs are fighting over whale meat.

KING PENGUINS CAN GO FOR MONTHS BETWEEN MEALS. ONE CHICK SURVIVED FOR FIVE MONTHS WITHOUT EATING.

This king penguin's nasty wound was inflicted by a leopard seal.

Snowy survivor

Penguins only feed in the sea, and can hunt their prey of fish at top speeds of 22 mph (35 km/h), appearing to almost fly through the water. Emperor penguins dive to depths of at least 1,740 ft (530 m) to reach fish, crustaceans, and squid. These birds have sharp-edged, hooked bills and their throats and tongues are coated with backward-pointing spines—features that ensure captured fish are on a oneway route to the stomach. Penguins face predation from seabirds, such as skuas, and leopard seals. One leopard seal may devour 12 Adélie penguins for a single meal.

DEATH SQUAD

There is not only safety in numbers—there is power. When animals work together to hunt and kill, they become a deadly force. Combining efforts means a successful hunt is more likely, and everyone gets a share of the kill. These death squads of the natural world have little to fear from predators or prey.

Lion's share

TWO LIONESSES WORK TOGETHER TO BACK A WILDEBEEST INTO A CORNER AND PREPARE TO STRIKE.

A pride of lions can dominate the landscape, invoking panic among nearby herds of herbivores. When it is time to feed, the primary hunters—the females—become more furtive. They stalk and surround their prey, constantly checking one another's position, before launching into the attack. Working together they can fell big prey, killing by sinking their teeth into the victim's windpipe, causing suffocation.

Canny canids

A PACK OF DOGS TARGETS A LONE WARTHOG, AND THE VICTIM DISAPPEARS ALMOST INSTANTLY IN THE FEEDING FRENZY.

Many dog species combine superb senses with cooperation, communication, and a strong social structure. African hunting dogs exemplify the canid lifestyle. They live in packs led by a dominant breeding pair, and hunt in groups of six to 20 animals. Their methods are brutal but efficient, pursuing a victim until it almost collapses with exhaustion, and taking opportunistic bites of flesh during the chase.

Killer whales

It has recently been discovered that orcas (killer whales) hunt in cooperative groups. These intelligent, adaptable animals will herd fish toward each other and then stun them with blows from their tail flukes. Against seals they employ a strategy known as "wave-hunting." Their ability to learn is key to their success—young orcas watch the hunt, and learn the technique.

1

WAVE-HUNTING

1. AT FIRST, THE GROUP OF ORCAS RAISE THEIR HEADS OUT OF THE WATER TO LOOK FOR SEALS RESTING ON ICE FLOES.

2

2. HAVING IDENTIFIED A TARGET, THE ORCAS SWIM AS A GROUP TOWARD AND BENEATH THE FLOE.

3. THIS CREATES A WAVE OR SWELL LARGE ENOUGH TO ROCK OR TIP THE FLOE, CAUSING THE SEAL TO FALL OFF THE ICE AND INTO THE ORCAS' WAITING MOUTHS.

3

SUPER POWERS

In the animal world, fantastical creatures and astounding stories of survival and savagery abound. From the murky bottom of the seabed to the dark interior of an insect's nest there are battles to be fought and won—and some of them involve extraordinary powers.

Little pistol shrimps may not look very impressive but these tiny marine crustaceans have a super power that packs a sonic punch. One claw is much bigger than the other—and this is the shrimp's secret weapon. As the claw is snapped shut a jet of water fires out at 60 mph (100 km/h), creating a bubble of superheated air in its wake. The bubble bursts, creating a loud cracking sound and a flash of light. The bang is powerful enough to stun, or even kill, prey.

CRACK!

PISTOL SHRIMP

A cuckoo wasp is able to infiltrate the nest of a beewolf (another type of wasp), lay its eggs, and escape—all without being detected. It achieves this incredible feat by means of an invisibility "cloak." The cuckoo wasp's skin is coated in chemicals that mimic the beewolf's own skin so closely that the beewolf thinks it is playing host to a member of its own family, not a trespasser. When the cuckoo wasp's eggs hatch, the larvae devour the beewolf's offspring.

SNEAK!

CUCKOO WASP

BOXER CRAB

KAPOW!

Small boxer crabs employ even tinier friends to help them become more brutal. They hold stinging sea anemones in their pincers and wave them about, like a boxer brandishing his gloved fists. By waving the anemones, the little pugilists show possible attackers that they are armed and ready. In return, the anemones feed on the crab's leftovers.

BOMBARDIER BEETLE

SQUIRT!

An explosive force can be a highly effective weapon, and animals knew this long before Alfred Nobel invented dynamite! Bombardier beetles combine liquids in their bodies to create a hot, toxic, and explosive liquid that they can aim at predators with incredible accuracy. Bombardier beetles are not the only insects to employ explosive defense methods: kamikaze termites and ants spontaneously rupture their bodies to release a toxic flare if their colony is in danger—but at least these bugs go out with a bang!

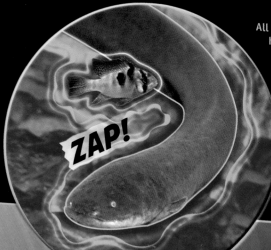

ZAP!

All animals have electricity in their bodies, but few have turned a normal life function into a killing force. Discharging electricity is called electrogenesis and electric eels are masters of the art. Despite their name these animals are not true eels, but a type of long-bodied fish, called a knifefish. Using up to 6,000 special "battery" cells on its abdomen, an electric eel can generate and store 600 volts, which it uses to stun or kill its prey.

ELECTRIC EEL

INDEX